D1491385

THE MADNESS OF
MODERN PARENTING

THE MADNESS OF
MODERN PARENTING
ZOE WILLIAMS

Contents

Preamble

Preamble

What it looks like from the outside…

FROM THE OUTSIDE, the madness looks like something modern parents do to themselves. It looks like martyrdom, self-righteousness, old-fashioned showing-off. They make such a big deal of it, from the minute they conceive. Immediately, they are repudiating cat faeces and mercury, things the rest of us hardly ever eat anyway. They can't just abstain from alcohol, they have to tell you endlessly how much they are abstaining, how important it is for the future of their progeny, how sacrificial it is of them, and yet, at the same time, incredibly easy, of course. Their buggies cost more than a second-hand car, and they huff and glare at you if you get in their way. It's impossible not to be in their way, because these buggies are also the size of a second-hand car. The world is in their way. They can't just breastfeed because they like it: it has to be a matter of life and death.

Everything is undertaken with this declamatory defiance, as though it is only their superiority, their learning, their altruism, their strength, standing between their baby and the infinite threat the world wilfully presents to it. Who died and made them the keeper of the species? How has humanity managed to keep itself alive this long without people being so preening and uptight about it?

And then it gets worse. When junior has graduated to eating food and sleeping normally, as all animals are wont, his or her every waking hour has to be filled with education and improvement. His or her progress must be chanted constantly; the boasting is shameless. All considerations of modesty and simple manners are instantly jettisoned, in favour of telling near strangers that you think your five-year-old might have an aptitude for Mandarin. Every hour must be distended to contain more opportunities for growth. It looks weirdly unnatural, lightless, this kind of parenting; I imagine it producing etiolated children, their knowledge incredibly long and thin.

How is it that parents managed perfectly well before – for centuries before – without this laboured intonation of 'It's the most important job in the world'? It has never been anything more or less important than it is right now. The sowing of your genetic seed in the soil of the future has never felt less vital than it does today. Excepting a bracket of the English upper class, nobody has ever wanted anything less than the best for their children; nobody has ever just shrugged their children off and not been that bothered. How do parents in the developing world today manage to raise children who, if they make it past cholera, become rounded adults without all that expertise? Why do today's parents have to make such an almighty fuss about everything?

What it feels like from the inside…

Then you get pregnant, and the first thing you realise, before – long before – you have any concept of 'baby', is this: the perfectionism and neurosis don't come from you. They come from outside.

I got pregnant with my first child in 2007. It wasn't a planned pregnancy – you're not allowed to say that when you have children; unfortunately, I already said it before he was born, so it's a matter of public record now. That being the case, I think it bears a bit of discussion. You're not allowed to say you didn't plan your pregnancy because people assume that means you love your child less than someone who did plan theirs. Everybody who has ever had a baby knows this is rubbish. An unplanned pregnancy is not the same as an unwanted pregnancy anyway. But even an unwanted pregnancy will, uninterrupted, turn into a wanted child. That's why adoption isn't the easy alternative to abortion: your pregnancy may have been an accident, but your baby is as desperately loved as anybody else's. Some people can conceptualise their baby before they meet it – and even love it before they meet it – but many people can't. I know *I* never did.

Then you have your baby, and you love him so much that you basically think he's the Messiah. Indeed, I think the whole nativity story – Jesus, the three kings, the donkeys, all of that – is just an extended metaphor for that moment of 'dark magic' (as the wonderful journalist Ariel Levy described it)[1] when you're hit by the force of maternity. I genuinely did think I'd just saved the world with my vagina. I was expecting the shepherds to arrive any minute.

---

1   'Thanksgiving in Mongolia', Ariel Levy, *New Yorker*, 18 November 2013.

Part 1

PROVOCATIONS

THE MADNESS OF MODERN PARENTING

ZOE WILLIAMS

SERIES EDITOR:
YASMIN ALIBHAI-BROWN

Biteback Publishing

First published in Great Britain in 2014 by
Biteback Publishing Ltd
Westminster Tower
3 Albert Embankment
London SE1 7SP
Copyright © Zoe Williams 2014

ISBN 978-1-84954-751-2

10 9 8 7 6 5 4 3 2 1

A CIP catalogue record for this book is available from the British Library.

Set in Stempel Garamond

Printed and bound in Great Britain by
CPI Group (UK) Ltd, Croydon CR0 4YY

MIX
Paper from
responsible sources
FSC® C020471
www.fsc.org

Part I

Advice, groupthink
and the evidence

THERE'S NOTHING INCOMPATIBLE about being an ambivalent pregnant person and a devoted mother. But because society is often daft – and people won't tell the truth about themselves for fear of society's off-beam, idiotic judgments – you don't often hear people say that they were ambivalent during gestation, in case the world thinks less of their bond with their babies. You can think of it as the parent trap, like a Chinese finger trap: inescapable even if you don't believe in it. You hear experts comment on maternal ambivalence, you hear a lot about it on *Woman's Hour* and you read beautiful novels about it;

but you rarely hear people say it of themselves. So the minute you get up the duff, in other words, you feel as though you're being policed inside out – not just inside your body, but inside your mind. And this, like any unwanted intrusion, leads to a lot of feelings of inadequacy, vulnerability, dissemblance and anger as you try to be the pregnant person the world wants you to be, where previously you were your own person who didn't care what the world wanted.

Oh yeah, also: I was horribly afflicted during pregnancy by something that I only read about last month with both my children now at school. How I wish I could go back in time and read about this before it happened. Pregnancy is, basically, a hyperinsulinic state,[2] which is to say your body deliberately lays down fat for the process and for the breastfeeding afterwards. The hormonal mechanism is that insulin interrupts your perception of the hormone leptin, which is what tells your brain that it's safe to stop eating and you can burn

---

2   *Fat Chance: The Hidden Truth About Sugar, Obesity and Disease*, Robert
    Lustig, Fourth Estate, 2014.

energy. Orexogenesis, the energy storage state, is sluggish; anorexogenesis, the energy burning state is, as you would expect, lively. This is true for all humans, but, naturally, we're also individuals; some people are hungrier and more sluggish in orexogenesis than others. Adolescence is another hyperinsulinic state, as you lay down fat for menstruation – become fertile, basically.

Now, I remember from adolescence that I am basically bovine in orexogenesis: all I can think about is food and sitting down. I remember one journey home from school when I bought a bar of chocolate at every sweet-shop I passed between Hammersmith and Wandsworth. For those who don't know London, this is 6 miles of prime retail real estate. I mean, sure, I was on a bus for some of them, but it was not pretty, this behaviour.

Anyway, I was exactly the same in pregnancy, famished and lazy from the word go. I couldn't walk past a Greggs. Every day, I ended up in tears of frustration about the crap I'd just eaten. Every other day, I'd hear some doctor, often a man but not always, pontificating about how you don't need extra calories until the third trimester because baby doesn't. The last thing baby needs is three sausage rolls and a slab of Tottenham cake. I remember the burning indignation at being told what to eat by somebody who had never been pregnant and had no idea how it felt. Couple that with burning indigestion and you can get some picture of my mood. I was in a terrible slough of despond – both times – for nine months. I put on 4 stone with my first child, didn't properly lose it afterwards, got pregnant again, put on another 4 stone. It was grimly hilarious with my second child, hearing midwives say how great it would be when the baby was born and I wouldn't feel so heavy: I was carrying 5.5 extra stone, of which my daughter composed only 9 pounds.

The short version of this story is that I was just not in the mood. I was not in the mood for cosy misinformation. I was not in the mood for being told what to do. I was definitely not in the mood for the patriarchy.

When did the world become so hazardous?

Risks during pregnancy are so overstated now that the British Pregnancy Advisory Service reports women requesting unnecessary abortions, which they don't want to have,[3] because they're so anxious about their alcohol intake in the period before they realised they were pregnant. The nutritional intake of pregnant women is fixated over, by everyone from new-agers to governments. (While I was pregnant, we were given £190 cash as a 'health in pregnancy grant' to spend on vegetables. It was canned by the coalition which, unusually, I agreed with. I don't know about you, but I certainly didn't spend it on vegetables.) There is some dispute about how close to starvation you can get while pregnant before your foetus is adversely affected; two studies of wartime famines in Russia and the Netherlands found, respectively, 'almost no effect' and 'some later-life effects'.[4] These were babies born from mothers who were on the point of starvation. The idea that you can harm your baby by not eating enough carrots is just preposterous.

The prohibitions have a slightly more medical

---

3   *The Independent*, Tuesday 7 October 2014.

4   The Dutch Famine Birth Cohort Study, L. H. Lumey et al., *International Journal of Epidemiology*, 2007; Fetal Programming and the Leningrad Siege Study, Stanner & Yudkin, 2001.

foundation, but only slightly. Immediately, the midwife ran me through the list of things I couldn't eat or drink, I smelt a rat. I actually said, 'I smell a rat', which she misheard for 'what about rat?' and, assuming that I was joking, said cheerfully: 'Definitely not rat!' It was sort of funny, except that I had actually had squirrel ballotine for lunch the day before, a slightly sadistic joke of the chef Richard Corrigan (not a joke on me, he didn't know me; a joke on any idiot who ordered it).

Raw egg, raw fish, raw meat, raw anything, tuna (raw or not), any cheese of any distinction, alcohol (clearly), stress and, by some interpretations, any complicated conversation. Suddenly, everything was banned. 'You get fat and you can't drink. It's the worst two things that can happen to a woman,' as my best friend had described it when it happened to her. Well, getting fat I was battling on with in my own particular way, but the rest … a lot of it just didn't make epidemiological sense. If, for instance, any alcohol at all would be toxic for a foetus, how is it that people of my generation, during whose gestations our mothers drank freely, are not marred by Foetal Alcohol Spectrum Disorder? If toxoplasmosis lived in the faeces of every cat, why did cat lovers never get smote down with it?

When we, the midwife and I, had finally established that I was being sceptical and not just surreal, she said: 'You can get listeriosis and not even know it until your baby has been born with a birth defect, you know.' Now, this is way, way off. Listeriosis is an extremely serious illness, somewhere in the region of Legionnaires' disease. If I'd got it, I would have been one of six pregnant women that year, one of four the next.[5] Not only would I notice, but the *Guinness Book of Incredibly Improbable Medical Events* would be on the phone too.

That's when I thought: there's something up with all this. Something has happened around the language, perception and presentation of danger in the area of parenting. Gestation and, I was soon to realise, early years – nought to three – have become minefields. Any misstep will cost you your healthy child. Stay alert, keep abreast, these missteps are everywhere. If you work hard enough,

---

5   http://webarchive.nationalarchives.gov.uk/20140714084352;
    http://www.hpa.org.uk/hpr/archives/2011/news1311.htm

put your own needs aside assiduously enough, you will be rewarded with the ultimate prize: a healthy baby. But one false move…

Doctors will always privately wave off these risks as possible but profoundly unlikely; and yet they will never come out and say so. That shot of real life, which has come to sound like unkempt nonchalance amidst the cacophony of drama queens, never makes it through to public debate. In fairness, what's in it for them? If you come out and say listeriosis is no big deal, you're the callous medic who doesn't care about babies. Professionals who break the code of extreme risk come in for needless, groundless attack. And for what? So some expectant mothers get to eat more cheese. It's just not worth the aggro.

But the result of this silence is that culture becomes more and more neurotic around pregnancy, to the extent that, by 2013, the Royal College of Obstetricians and Gynaecologists (RCOG) was advising women not to sit on new furniture or eat from a new frying pan.[6] Again,

---

6   https://www.rcog.org.uk/globalassets/documents/guidelines/5.6.13chemic
    alexposures.pdf

the approach was weird: they had no evidence of what environmental chemicals did to a baby's development. 'For most environmental chemicals we do not know whether or not they really affect a baby's development, and obtaining definitive guidance will take many years,' the executive summary said. 'This paper outlines a practical approach that pregnant women can take, if they are concerned.'

Now, there is so much wrong with that statement – either these things are harmful or they aren't. If they are, they should be banned. If we don't know but think they probably are, they should be banned while we find out. If we don't know, but think they probably aren't, then everyone should just stop worrying. Instead, this peels off a certain, superior kind of mother – the one who is 'concerned' – and offers her 'practical tips' that actually aren't practical at all. (How on earth would you check whether your food had been cooked in a new frying pan? What if your existing frying pan breaks during pregnancy? I guess someone could start up a second-hand frying pan exchange, but still...)

The end result is that risk is removed from the public

domain – an environmental chemical can only be dealt with at a legislative level – and re-cast as an individual responsibility. And all this, not just with the collusion, but at the *active behest*, of the most important obstetric body in the country. So, some pregnant women – probably most – ignore the advice and are cast as the less concerned, less responsible ones, whose babies' birth defects, should they arise, could have been averted had they been more cautious. Other pregnant women, those who are 'concerned', arouse suspicion and hostility, with the watching world thinking (and often saying): 'Jesus, these pregnant women, with their attention-seeking obsessions, their irrational dreads. How am I supposed to know how old the sofa is?' If an equivalent statement were made in the non-pregnant world – 'We do not know if nitrogen dioxide is carcinogenic, but those who are concerned should live away from bus routes' – we would, quite rightly, rebel: 'No, I will not live away from a bus route. Sort out your stupid buses.'

Anyway, I wrote all this in a column – in a nutshell: 'Obstetric professionals, I do not believe your bullshit about cheese' – and one doctor, wearing a metaphorical tin hat, came out to support it. His name was (is) Professor Eric Jauniaux, and, during my time milking him for medical back-up, he left his incredibly high-achieving career at UCL to teach basic midwifery skills in the developing world. I never did figure out whether the reason he broke ranks to say 'this is all nonsense' was because he had seen the coalface of what childbirth looks like when it really is dangerous, or just because he is French. Whatever. This is what he wrote (for clarity, PubMed[7] is a collected source of peer-reviewed papers in medical journals):

Listeria and pregnancy – Google, 190,000 hits; PubMed, 107 hits. Cheese and listeria – Google, 194,000 hits; PubMed, 169 hits. Sushi and pregnancy – Google, 628,000 hits; PubMed, zero hits. Raw fish and listeria: Google, 123,000 hits; PubMed, 49 hits. You can see immediately the disproportion between the epidemiological evidence and the general public hysteria about the disease.

7   http://www.ncbi.nlm.nih.gov/pubmed

He said he had attended a conference of bacteriologists that year, and not one of them had encountered a case of listerioris in the past decade.

And yet, at least this scare has the distinction of actually being true: if you did eat unpasteurised cheese, and you were the unluckiest person ever to live (of the last ten listeriosis outbreaks in America, only two were from cheese, and one of those was a Mexican homemade cheese … that gives you some indication of how unlucky you would have to be), then you would certainly be at risk of spontaneous abortion or brain-damaging your foetus.

The same cannot be said of the conflicting instructions around piffling amounts of alcohol; this is where advice diverges recklessly from evidence.

In May 2007, while I was still pregnant, the Department of Health settled on a message of complete abstinence from alcohol. This was in spite of the fact that they could find no evidence of harm at levels below 1.5 units per day. Nobody has ever found evidence of harm at low-to-moderate levels of drinking. A few ridiculous studies, where researchers rang a bell over the pregnant belly at twenty-eight weeks, despite the fact that there is no basis to believe movements are voluntary or foe-tuses can hear at this age, have found that the babies of teetotallers are more lively. But across a broad range of reputable research, study after study has found that alcohol is fine, except in large doses, which makes sense in the light of Jauniaux's point: 'Alcohol is mainly metabolised by the liver, and only what's left will be met by the placenta. The amount that could reach the foetus in a glass of beer or a glass of wine is negligible. I would be much more concerned with breastfeeding and drinking.' He's a placental transfer specialist, incidentally.[8] Not just any old obstetrician.

It's always possible that he was simply a maverick, one of those people who will push a point, overstate a case, just to be the person who overstated the case, the person whose name people remember. Eric Jauniaux was not that person: senior as he was, he was in charge of high-risk pregnancies at UCL. As time went on, I met more and more people who had been under his treatment during

---

8   Which is to say, his research is into how nutrients and other substances pass from woman to foetus.

pregnancy. A school friend of mine said that, when she was pregnant, she asked him about alcohol and he looked her straight in the eye and said: 'You should probably draw the line at about a bottle of whisky a day.' Just imagine: a doctor, treating you like a human being, giving advice one adult to another, complete with a sense of humour and the understanding that you weren't a total idiot. Just imagine that. So last century.

In October 2007, the National Institute for Health and Care Excellence (NICE) put it out to consultation and, in March 2008, came back with a new message: 'Do not drink any alcohol.' Or, if you decide to drink alcohol, only drink some alcohol. This included some notes, of which these two are my favourite:

> 1. Last year the Department of Health commissioned the National Perinatal Epidemiology Unit to undertake a review of existing national and international evidence on the effects of alcohol on the developing embryo, foetus and child. The principal findings were that there is no consistent evidence that low-to-moderate consumption of alcohol during pregnancy has any adverse effects,

although there is some evidence that binge drinking can affect neurodevelopment of the foetus.

2. While scientific basis for our advice has not changed, the evidence base is not extensive and we believe it is possible the previous advice could be misinterpreted by some that it is safe to drink 'a little' when pregnant, where 'a little' can differ from person to person. Most women do actually stop drinking or drink very little in pregnancy, so a slightly stronger message is aimed at those who do not reduce their consumption to appropriate levels.

To turn that into normal language: there is no evidence, but there's no point telling women to drink 'a little'; all the sensible ones will have stopped drinking anyway and the rest won't understand what 'a little' means. I rang the Department of Health to put it to them that this tack – advice for which there is no evidence – was unbefitting of governmental intervention. An audibly young man told me, 'Yes, but the situation is slightly different because most women want to do the best for their baby.'

In 2013, UK advice went back to 'no alcohol'. At around this time, the American economist Emily Oster published her book, *Expecting Better*, in which she number-crunched the risks surrounding pregnancy to determine which of them made sense.[9] She found the alcohol guidelines the most ridiculous, for exactly the same reason obtained six years before: there was just no evidence for it. She wrote:

> One phrase I kept coming across was 'no amount of alcohol has been proven safe' … this seemed to me to have two problems. First, too much of any goods can be bad. If you have too many bananas, the excess potassium can be a real problem. But no doctor is going around saying 'no amount of bananas have been proven safe!' … Second, what is all this evidence if not proof? It's exactly this type of evidence that leads us to conclude that binge drinking is problematic. But if you are willing to conclude that, why wouldn't you be willing to conclude that light drinking is fine? That is what the evidence shows.

---

9   *Expecting Better*, Emily Oster, Orion, 2013.

What interested me from this distance was that, while the evidence hadn't changed, the vitriol had. People attacked Oster for having the audacity to try and interpret medical data with only an economist's training. People accused her of creating unnecessary cases of FASD[10] – apparently women who, previously, would have abstained from alcohol, might read a book by an American economist and get pissed all the way through pregnancy instead. People accused her of causing brain damage in her own daughter. In the half-decade that had passed, it had become markedly less acceptable to question the presentation of risk around childbearing. And again, the deathly silence. Whole continents of medics who could easily say, 'She's right about the data,' but wouldn't.

Why won't they? Is it cowardice, professional protectionism? I think we're witnessing the import of an American medical culture – wherever they can offload risk from themselves onto you, they do. I don't blame them, in a way, because it's a litigious, market-based

---

10 Foetal Alcohol Spectrum Disorder.

system that has no room for luck, happenstance and genetic misfortune. But it's not a system I think we need here. I would prefer to see trust between medics and patients.

Liquid gold: the breastmilk fallacy

This morning, messing about on Twitter, I followed a link to a headline from *The Onion*: 'Scientists find link between people who breastfeed and people who think they know what's best for everybody.'[11] Look, it's not notable because it's funny – *The Onion* is always funny – what's notable is that this is still a thing when the case for breastfeeding has been made. If the people making that case were reasonable, they would accept that the information has been transmitted. Everybody knows it's better for baby. They would accept that some people, for whatever reason (probably their own inadequacy), couldn't do it, or wouldn't. Then the 'breast is

---

11 http://www.theonion.com/articles/
   new-study-finds-link-between-breastfeeding-always,36823/

best' charabanc would move on and women wouldn't have to feel so guilty five years after their children were onto solids.

But breastfeeding proselytisers never do move on; they are always at it, driving people with their rigidity and certainties. And what's really infuriating is that a lot of it isn't even true. Benefits that are unproven or minor are amplified ridiculously.[12] Figures put out by the Department of Health – or bodies sponsored by the DH – are lifted from data collected in Honduras. If you dare to say any of this – formula milk *is* dangerous, but only in countries without clean water, and anyone trying to transpose that guilt onto UK mothers is having a laugh – the rage is immense.

I chaired a debate (about something quite different: health visitors) for the Royal College of Midwives in 2010, and breastfeeding activists threatened a demonstration outside it. I had to wear a mac in case I got

---

12 Read the paragraph entitled 'Limitations': 'Because all these studies are observational, it is not possible to rule out the possibility that effects may be partly explained by self-selection of mothers who breastfeed.' Or, indeed, wholly explained thereby.

egged. They didn't demonstrate. Two of them turned up and looked tight-lipped in the sixth row. Their beef was that anybody who says publicly that the case for breastfeeding has been overblown shouldn't be allowed anywhere near the institutions of childbirth. Even if I'm right (which I am), it's the wrong message: it's not 'supportive' to mothers, which makes me the wrong person to be allowed to speak to mothers. The ridiculous thing is I absolutely loved breastfeeding and I would have done it even if there were evidence in the opposite direction showing that it caused ear infections or made the baby's IQ go down. Nevertheless, when the evidence for breastfeeding was so hopelessly poor, so uncontrolled for social factors, so exaggerated and so undisciplined, it seemed to be important to say so.[13]

Now, the older reader might say: this was a key issue in the feminist movement, getting women to breastfeed. In the '70s, the question was: how can we reclaim women's bodies so that our breasts are seen not just as

---

13   The really courageous voice here is Joan Wolf, in *Is Breast Best?*, NYU Press, 2010.

objects of sexual gratification, but as a way to feed our own children for our own elemental gratification? That lobby was just as fierce, to be fair. Women who dared to express any regret at the loss of sexual identity following motherhood, for reasons related to breastfeeding, were booed out of feminist bookshops (more on that later).

But what's happened now is that all the ferocity of the feminist argument has been marshalled into something quite different: a way of controlling women with the orthodoxy of how they should – if they are proper mothers – behave. I think of the middle-class women I've interviewed or known as friends, who couldn't get along with breastfeeding and yet felt that they couldn't be 'proper' mothers without it. Most of them just battle through miserably, frozen cabbage leaves in their bras, pointless wheat-free diets, waiting it out. A friend went to a lactation workshop and just ripped her top off, bared her two bright red breasts to a room full of strangers, going, 'Look! Look at this! What am I supposed to do with this?' and everybody rushed soothingly towards her, trying to get her back in her clothes, assuring her that it was perfectly normal to be in pain so outrageous that the memory of labour was like a warm bath. Seriously, even if it were the liquid gold it's cracked up to be, this simply wouldn't be right. Mothers are people too. To make a nutritional compromise is not the end of the world.

But it also causes a rift between the classes that I think is totally unnecessary – the path of rectitude is now, by coincidence, also the path that is mainly taken by richer women. The more affluent you are, the more likely you are to breastfeed, and that, I imagine, is a combination of factors: the cultural norms you've experienced; the people you respect; whether you can afford to get someone else to take your toddler off your hands when you have a new baby; how soon you have to go back to work; whether or not you have to rely on other people to feed your baby; how much time you have to lie in bed. It's quite a leisurely activity. You can't do it while you're ironing (though I did once do it while getting some sausages out of the oven). There is such a plain link between infant feeding and the class you're in that a lot of mothers who don't breastfeed feel like other mothers, indeed, other people, are looking down on them as social inferiors. And they don't feel like that because they're mad – they're right. So this precious, evanescent time when you feel a bond with people, not because they share a background or interests or hobbies, but because they have a baby the same age and you know they're feeling exactly the same things you are, is polluted by rules and stratification that are totally unnecessary.

Pregnancy: rules and roulette

Crucially, in our new risk-averse culture, what's missing is any proportionality. We live now as if in a binary position: things are either safe for baby or dangerous for baby. This whole business has become a game of whist, in which risk trumps sense. Anybody claiming to be motivated by the safety of the baby automatically silences anybody motivated by evidence. When I was in the business of producing babies, it used to make me livid, whereupon well-meaning people would say, 'Have you ever thought of what this stress is doing to your baby?' (The answer is nothing. Yet again, studies showing severe stress causing damage to a foetus have been extrapolated to form the assumption that slight stress will cause slight damage, even though no slight damage has ever been shown. Not to mention the question of how slight stress is even measured.)

Now I'm out of the woods, I still feel keenly that something important has happened, some shift towards rigidity that people never previously found necessary. It's a new world out there, where you prove your fitness as a parent by being as neurotic as you possibly can, and you place yourself way outside the mainstream by asking questions about evidence, overstatement and room for manoeuvre, which in the rest of life would be commonplace.

In the past, I was always scratching around for a feminist interpretation – people are saying these things in order to subjugate women, to re-domesticate us, to make us insecure in our own judgements, to patronise us, to make us feel that we can't evaluate risk factors on our own. That was just the way I was accustomed to dealing with things: if a situation doesn't make sense, if you're being blamed for something that you couldn't have controlled (think sexual assault), if it feels as though your instincts are being manipulated in order to deliver up your obedience, well, most likely, this is all to do with the patriarchy.

And while I cleave to that in all kinds of other situations, in parenting I don't think it's so: I think the new 'danger culture' manipulates mothers and fathers equally, for reasons unrelated to gender. I think the change goes to the bedrock of society, though whether that is above or below sexism, I wouldn't care to judge.

Part II

Part II

The baby

The baby

AND THEN THE baby, give or take a few hours in the warzone, comes out.

What a precious and awe-inspiring time it is once you're out of the grip of hocus pocus, once everything is fine, once you are either breastfeeding or have made your peace with not breastfeeding. When I write new baby cards for people now I can never think of anything to say, because all I want to say is, 'You bastards. I'm so jealous,' and, irrationally, it seems inappropriate to swear on a card for a baby. If you are lucky, you might spend the first six months so blissed out that you won't even notice the battle for perfect parent going on around you, a fight that is roughly as fierce as the Hunger Games. But sooner or later, you will notice.

First comes attachment – 'hugger mother' versus 'scheduler mother'. Fathers can join in too; attachment theorists are always at pains to point out that a single caregiver can be male or female, so long as it's always them giving the care. We think of it as a battle between women, because those who draw its lines blame everything on women.

In a nutshell – and it's pretty simple, you don't need much more than a nutshell – hugger mothers respond to their baby's every need, and scheduler mothers get babies into a routine, so that they don't have to guess at their needs. If it's noon, it must be hungry. If it's lonely, it must be Tuesday. Everything has a timetable, and if it happens at that time, you know where to look.

The saddest and most vivid articulation of this debate was seen on *This Morning* last year. Peaches Geldof, the hugger mother, was debating Katie Hopkins, the timetabler. Geldof described the 'seven Bs', which are breastfeeding, birth bonding, bedding with baby, baby wearing, believing your baby's cry, bewaring people who want you to mistrust your baby, and another one about bonding that she couldn't remember. Geldof, beautiful and beatific, was impossible not to love. I don't believe in searching for maternal perfection (I think that's probably already come across), but, nevertheless, that doesn't mean that when I hear somebody passionately and sincerely defending their way of doing things I don't fall for them a bit. She spoke with the voice of urgent empathy, a person digging into the farthest reaches of her heart to figure out what her sons were trying to tell her with their warbling and yelling. She was on a mission to make sure she understood them and that they knew they were understood.

Hopkins responded with bizarre cruelty. 'It's all a bit knit-your-own-Birkenstocks,' she started off, before accusing Geldof of knitting her own yoghurt and fashioning more Birkenstocks some other way. 'A-P, attachment parenting,' she concluded, 'it's just one step away from C-R-A-P, crap parenting.' She sounded rattled and wildly irrelevant. Moreover, she sounded quite angry. Now, that's practically her raison d'être – the ability to sound angry at everything in a totally unfair and disproportionate way – so maybe we shouldn't read too much into it. But there's an underlying truth here which is that when we hit these inevitable fault lines in the maternal ideal – they're inevitable because even looking for an ideal is a false project – the upshot is usually one woman bitching at another.

A while before I had children, in the early '00s, I was asked to review a book of 'comebacks' – what to say if you're a stay-at-home mother and a working mother is rude to you. It was a pretty short book, more of a toilet read, but there was one classic line: 'When she calls you unintelligent, reply, "At least I was clever enough to find a husband who could keep me."' I thought (indeed, I think I said in the review): these women are all mad. If this is what parenting turns you into, maybe we should give it a rest for a generation, leave it to French people.

Aside from the rank improbability of the above conversation ever occurring – we tend not to call each other stupid to our faces – it distilled the trajectory of this cultural snakepit. Instead of saying, 'Well, why do women who look after their own kids feel denigrated, while women who go back to work feel judged as bad mothers?'; instead of asking, 'What are the currents of misogyny, authority and scapegoating beneath all that?', we just set the two camps against one another. It's like dropping two fighter ferrets into a cage by their tails. That's what happened on *This Morning*.

Everything about it is tragic, it's much too painful to watch – from the great lost reservoirs of Geldof's maternal love, which her sons will only know in the abstract, to the awful inevitability of Hopkins's personality as she turns herself into a piñata because she'd rather people hated her than didn't pay her attention – and then argues that the last thing babies need is attention.

Once again, I find myself torn between being a natural hugger mother, and hating the self-righteousness that the huggers exhibit, along with the sheer self-abnegating impracticality to which it often amounts. Attachment theory, in its most thoughtful incarnation,[14] is utterly alive to difference: the difference between one baby and another; between one mother and another; between motherhood at one time of life and at another; between mothers and fathers (but also the similarities therein). It is keenly aware of social and economic interference into that critical love

14 *Nurturing Natures*, Graham Music, Psychology Press, 2010.

affair, and would never make it a moral superiority of one mother, the successful hugger, over another, who had to schedule because she had to get back to work. Some of the most evocative, empathetic, emboldening work ever written about parenthood comes from the Bowlby tradition.[15]

However, like so many strains of parenting, this has become a purist's playground, with no room for compromise. There is no longer any such thing as a bearable imperfection or common sense. You can't go back to work and put your baby in a nursery – the impacts will ricochet into his or her entire adult psyche. Least of all can you go back to work because you enjoy work. There is some allowance made for mothers who have post-natal depression – you're allowed to outsource your baby for a bit if it's making you want to commit suicide – but anybody who isn't on the brink of a mental breakdown should just knuckle down and attach, breast-feeding exclusively for the first six months, and partially

---

15 Bowlby was a seminal British psychoanalyst who developed Attachment Theory in the '50s and '60s, starting with the infant's need to attach to one person and for that bond to be responsive and constant.

until the child is two (as guidelines now suggest). The Geldof–Hopkins row is evocative for larger reasons than the separate tragedies of the protagonists: it is utterly typical of the way parenting is constructed in our culture. You take an act – loving your baby – that any normal person would imagine can have infinite forms of expression, and try to codify it into two oppositional, mutually exclusive states.

As much as the proponents of one side or the other try to inject some subtlety, the way the argument is set up is for demolition, not compromise, and certainly not to take good bits from each perspective and turn it into a workable patchwork that might differ from person to person. Inevitably, after the careful removal of any nuance, both sides end up pretty cartoonish and the viewer is invited to choose who's right on the basis of who they like the most. Really, it's pretty damn hard to present a likeable face in this kind of arena: when it comes down to it, you're choosing who you hate, and then de facto agreeing with their opponent. 'Mine enemy's enemy is my friend' is the abiding principle.

The most glaring problem with it is that it totally ignores

any of the economic imperatives that beset many parents. Attachment, along with breastfeeding fundamentalism, enshrines a parenting ideal that actually excludes quite a significant proportion of the population. Women on low incomes tend not to take even six months of maternity leave; the assumption has to be that it is money chasing them back to work and not just some coincidence whereby lower-paid women are less bonded with their babies than their higher-paid counterparts. Statutory maternity pay is far too low to live on[16] and 49 per cent of children in two London boroughs are born below the poverty line.[17] There's been a surge in self-employment over the past three years (there's a story behind that, but that'll have to wait for some other time), with average wages that are extremely low.[18] It is really improbable that people on self-employed wages could save enough to take even four months off.

---

16 http://workingflex.wordpress.com/2014/03/17/
    1500-nappies-nct-reveals-cost-of-the-parent-penalty/

17 http://www.cpag.org.uk/content/london-has-highest-child-poverty-rate

18 http://www.taxresearch.org.uk/Documents/SEI2013.pdf

So we have an ideal creeping into our collective under-standing of what maternal and/or parental love looks like, which a lot of people just can't afford. (And all the benefits of baby bonding evaporate when you look at scrounger rhetoric: if you stay at home to tend your baby while you're on benefits, suddenly that has noth-ing to do with your bonding. Instead, you're work-shy.)

This is the critical problem: enshrining parental love into a series of distinct, identifiable markers (bonding, believing, breastfeeding etc.) that people who have to work will simply have less time for than people who don't. It's a slippery slope from there to the assump-tion that poor people are just not as good at loving their children as rich ones and, if that sounds extreme, those assumptions are already visible in early-years policy documents.

Political parenting

The Labour MP Graham Allen produced a report with Iain Duncan Smith, 'Early Intervention: Good Par-ents, Great Kids, Better Citizens', in which the authors talk of the things that parents need to know – how to 'recognise and respond to a baby's cues, attune with infants and stimulate them from the very start, and how to foster empathy' (at this point, nobody was suggesting universal parenting classes; some sorts of parent were considered to be born with these skills). Allen mentions parents being 'ill-informed and poorly motivated', but he doesn't specify any particular, observed parents. Iain Duncan Smith wrings his hands about poor parenting, then suggests that disability benefit should be taxed. The 'problem families' tsar, Louise Casey, periodically releases statements bemoaning the personal inadequacy of families whose real lack is of money and support. Maybe they do lack inner resources, maybe they are depressed, maybe they are fatigued, but I'd love to see a person who isn't while earning their poverty on miserable wages and being hectored about their parenting. Only Aptamil has anything good to say to mothers: 'The job's yours. You're doing it brilliantly.' It's a schmaltzy marketing ploy that just happens to be true.

Parents who had their children some years hence, or people who've never been parents, will regard this with bafflement – since when did humans need to be 'motivated' to respond to their babies? Since when did 'information' foster empathy? And yet, if you're within this parenting cycle, you will recognise immediately the language of the game: 'motivated' and 'informed' stand in for 'people like you'; the 'unmotivated' and 'ill-informed' are some other sorts of people. The report concludes: 'Many parents are doing a brilliant job, but in some homes the child is strapped in a pushchair and pointed at a blank wall during those precious, irreplaceable first two or three years. It is a wasted opportunity, for which they and we pay the price over successive years.'

It's unreferenced and, of course, that pathetic pushchair mother is unidentified. I've had this argument a ton of times in public and academic meetings. Who are these terrible parents who don't know how to bond? What does it say about our policy environment that we're citing them, with no evidence, as a real social problem we can't prove but all know is there? And someone[19]

---

19 One time it was Helen Reece, who wrote this interesting, though tangential, chapter, 'The pitfalls of positive parenting', *Ethics and Education*, 8(1), 2013, pp. 42–54.

always says: 'But these parents do exist; there are people who simply aren't caring for their children properly.' Of course this is true. I have slowly realised what I'm objecting to: it's not the idea that all parents may not be perfect, and some parents may need help, but rather, that there is a coded attempt to stratify inadequate parenting by class. It is never said out loud that the pushchair mum is poor, but if she were a middle-class mother, nobody would have seen her toddler staring at a wall. She never would have been earmarked for 'intervention'. (Professor of Social Work, Sue White, said once: 'Intervention, horrible word. Who wants to be intervened with? People want to be helped.')

In other words, the middle-class mother would never be accused of creating a social problem, because she wouldn't start off in the group whose behaviour is considered the wellspring of social problems. The main causes of failure to bond (or empathise) are depression, tiredness and addiction. Poverty is a risk factor for drug use, but everything else is class-blind. The presentation of this issue, in other words, is completely wrong. If there are parents who aren't coping, they need help, but if we persist with the idea that all problems spring from a certain type of family, then that help won't reach the right people and it won't feel like help.

However, when you go into battle over what is essentially the construction of a new class prejudice, you often find yourself fighting with the wrong people. I've lost count of the number of times I've become embroiled in a row with a psychotherapist, to whom attachment theory isn't a politician's yardstick, it's a life's quest to comprehend the foundations of the self. A lot of the deeper questions about how nurturance happens, and what it does, are fascinating, but they are very often torpedoed by a different agenda.

Let's leave the pushchair-and-blank-wall parent and return to the perfect parent. Such is the wider economic situation that the number of women who can't spend as much time with their babies as they'd like is by no means limited to the very lowest paid. The National Childcare Trust (NCT) produced some research this year that showed nearly half of women returning to work before they wanted to, either because they ran out of money, or because they were concerned about job security.[20] Of those women, how many will be able to replace themselves with optimal caregivers? Very few. A nanny would cancel out the median wage altogether; grandparent care tends to be free but you're damn lucky if it's on hand. What you see developing here is not an underclass who can't afford to do it right, but rather, women in huge numbers having to make decisions for economic rather than parental reasons, all the while keenly aware that the only motivation they can publicly own up to is 'what's best for baby'.

This creates a culture of guilt and self-hate, which finds its expression in these toxic rows between one archetypal mother and another. It isn't that long ago – it's within living memory – that parenthood was more of a mixed bag. I remember a time when people valued parents and children for their resilience, and there was broad understanding of how hard it was. People did things differently without hating one another for doing things differently simply because they were different people.

---

20 http://www.nct.org.uk/press-release/nct-research-finds-women-are-ending-maternity-leave-sooner-they-would

People accepted that sometimes they had to do things for the money, without having to accept that they were less of a parent as a result.

If it's become bizarrely taboo to admit that your parenting sometimes has to come second to earning a living, one thing has become even more unsayable: that you might want to go to work, even after you've had a baby, because you enjoy it. This is as open-and-shut a feminist issue as you could get, and it's one in which the mainstream understanding of equality has gone hurtling backwards. Nobody would question the fitness of a father who continued to find his work rewarding after the birth of a child. Indeed, I've noticed a nauseating return of the approving breadwinner narrative, where fathers work *harder* after baby comes along, which is all well and good because clearly he's thinking about the security of the family. WAKE UP! He's just trying to get out of doing bedtime, as any sane person would who'd spent all day at work and was perhaps a little noise sensitive.

Yet a mother who wants to go back to her job when her baby is seven months old, not for the money, just because she enjoys her work … well, that is something mothers just cannot admit. In my experience, women have no trouble admitting this to each other. We'll admit that we always find work easier and sometimes find it more rewarding than looking after children. (Especially those who are pre-speech – the babies, I mean, not the mothers. We are more like post-speech.) We'll admit that we miss our workplace identities, not to mention our friends, and sometimes do not find it that exciting sitting in Starbucks talking about cradle cap. We'll admit that we do work that brings in no money at all (once childcare is taken out) just to get away from our own stinking children (and houses). And we'll admit that the experience of looking after children is very intense, but not always in a good way. Sometimes it's intensely frustrating, or boring.

Look around at the way motherhood is discussed in the public sphere, however, and you'll see two distinct pictures – contradictory, incompatible, similar only insofar as they are both wrong.

On the one hand, it is taken as given that all women have their identity overwritten by childbirth and thenceforward only want to be mothers, for as long as the workplace can possibly spare them and for as long as they can get away with. We've gone from a culture in which women think it's really clever to get back to work with fresh stitches, with no outward sign that anything happened to them, to this: a culture in which women take maternity leave competitively, and the higher your status, the more you can take.

On the other hand, politics describes parenthood as a conundrum for think tanks to solve. In this version, the party that comes up with the cheapest wraparound childcare option, where you can shunt your baby into nursery or your child into 8 a.m.–6 p.m. school (all the better to resume your productivity as an economic unit), will win the 'family vote'.

There is no room in either of these pictures for the mother who doesn't want her child to be in a big crowd twelve hours a day before it can even speak, but likewise doesn't want to entirely relinquish her own place in the world. There's no comprehension at all from politics that you might want to be with your children for the sheer thrill of being with them, but also get away from them because you did, after all, remain an adult, and you still need adult pursuits. It's like a conversation designed by a robot: either the child is at the centre, and the mother has ceased to be a whole person, or economic productivity is at the centre, and the child is merely a time-management issue that the right policy will be able to take care of. The party that solves this will be the party that realises it's not up to them to solve it. It's up to them to make sure parents are paid well enough, and treated well enough, that they have the power to solve it themselves. Weirdly, in this arena again, one often finds oneself arguing with the wrong people. So, I might say, 'I don't want to put my kids into breakfast club and after-school club, and return home to find they've had a longer day than I have,' and the person who is really riled by that will be the one who's *had* to do that because otherwise she or he would lose their job. Suddenly, I'm the self-righteous prick making them feel bad about their parenting; and nobody is looking at the world and saying: 'Hang on, we have a political culture that glorifies parenting on the one hand, and yet creates economic pressures that actively separate us from our children on the other.'

Follow the money

Wherever you see a trend that makes no human sense, there's always somebody, somewhere, making a lot of money out of it. The baby market – equipment, transport, safety, furniture and feeding products – is worth £900 million a year. That astonished me. When I first read it, I thought it meant children's products and covered the years nought to eighteen. Nope – that's just for babies. The more intense the risk aversion is, the more money there is to be made from it. Buggies are the obvious example, with new hazards dreamt up every year to warrant the purchase of a thousand-pound chariot. The reasons you can't just plop them in a second-hand Maclaren are legion. If they're not facing you, they won't learn to empathise. If you haven't got the right kind of foam, they'll get a flat head. Childhood is a huge testbed for innovation. You just have to look at the trunki and the microscooter to see that. (If you don't know what these are: microscooters are those maddening contraptions that bash you in the ankles when under the command of a two-year-old who can barely even stay upright; trunkis are those infuriating suitcases that you trip over in airports.) But babyhood is more like a testbed for exploiting the desperate.

Take sleep: parents would do anything for sleep. Babies who won't sleep defy the laws of biology. Even the big ones need sixteen hours sleep a day, and yet, against the odds, some of them get by on two. I have friends in their forties whose parents still talk about how little they slept. This is not an impossible quandary; there are things you can do that they teach you in sleep clinics, so long as you are dogged, immovable, desperate and have some blackout blinds. But they won't always work, and the problem won't always be bad enough for referral to a sleep clinic. Even when it is bad enough, you probably won't get referred for a few months, by which time the problem has often gone away. Into this huge breach – the parents whose problem is not quite bad enough for a referral, but is easily bad enough to ruin their lives and make them want to kill each other – steps entrepreneurship. Ewan the dream sheep or slumber bear are cuddly toys with special features – a 'heartbeat' or some such. They usually retail at around £30 – enough to make people think they might do something; not enough that they will engage their critical brain.

The pure, wishful-thinking nonsense underlying it all has been going on since the beginning of time. When you get a puppy, lore tells you to wrap an alarm clock and a hotwater bottle in a towel, and it will think it's still with its mother. It is shamelessly wrong. No puppy in the history of time has mistaken a towel with a clock in it for its mother. I know; I have checked with dogs. And yet, some bead of truth lurks in there, the sense that there must be an answer, there simply must. Into that faith in the universe steps the maker of a cuddly toy that doesn't work. Parents drop hundreds of pounds on this nonsense. I remember a friend telling me, while I was pregnant, to be wary of the new gadgets you see in Mothercare. I asked for an example, and she said:

> Well, you can get these babywipe warmers, battery-operated heat pads that you keep your wipes on, so that when you use one, they're nice and warm. And it actually is quite nice, when you accidentally leave your wipes on the radiator, to think that you're not giving the

baby a horrible shock with a cold wipe. But really, it's ridiculous, isn't it?

I thought: you are dead right, that's ridiculous. It's the most ridiculous thing I've ever heard. But when the baby was right there, in that tender state, I did sometimes think: if only I didn't have to shock him with this room-temperature wipe.

Gripped by a perpetual fear that something might go wrong, you'll buy anything. This is the only possible explanation for the Sproutling, a tagging device that you put round your baby's ankle while it's asleep that transmits data to your iPhone, telling you what the light and temperature is in the room, as well as how the baby's heart rate is doing. Room temperature is a constant torment to new parents. One of the worst arguments I ever had was during a feverish (my fever, not the baby's) attempt to keep the baby's room cool. An overly hot room is thought to cause Sudden Infant Death Syndrome.

My fella said, 'What this room needs is a through-put of air.'

'RUPERT THE BEAR?' I yelled. 'How is a Rupert the Bear going to help? You idiot.'

That story is by-the-by. I just thought it was a useful indication of what sleep deprivation plus anxiety can do to a person, which might in turn illuminate the discussion as to why anyone would spend £180 on a Sproutling.

The wisdom of ancients

The *Daily Mail*, somewhat ironically, reported a finding recently that 70 per cent of parents felt judged by other people on the quality of their parenting.[21] I call that ironic because it had the subtext of 'poor parents, feeling so judged', when the paper itself is the main generator of public disapprobation since the Calvinist church. But whatever. Who said newspapers had to be consistent?

Fathers feel that most of this unbidden criticism comes

---

21 http://www.dailymail.co.uk/femail/article-2676671/70-parents-feel-judged-decisions-make-child-three-quarters-given-advice-without-asking-it.html

from other parents. Mothers agree to a point, but feel the scrutiny weighs more heavily upon them when it comes from the generation above – specifically, mothers-in-law and mothers.

Mothers and mothers-in-law often don't express their disapproval because they know that it's not the done thing. I realise I'm pretty fortunate in that – neither my mother nor my fella's would ever say, openly, that they disagreed with a decision, although my mother-in-law's face was a picture when I spent the first six months of my son's life feeding him every time he made a noise.

Where they will pipe up, though, is on the consumer angle. They won't say to your face, 'I think you're feeding him too much sugar/not enough roughage,' but they will say, 'I don't know why you've bought that absurd baby gym, in our day, we just used to tie a can to the ceiling and put you underneath it.'

It doesn't help that they've got terrible memories. It's absolutely maddening, the things they'll tell you as fact: that you ate the end of a French loaf when you were six weeks old (they must mean six months … or six years?); that they never used to bother with pureeing, because you were born with teeth; that you once gave a builder directions to the A302, even though you were only two, had never been in a car, and didn't even live on the right side of London. I only point that out for mischief. It has no bearing on what I'm about to say.

Your mother can tell you're doing things differently to the way she did them, and often she doesn't really approve of your new way. However, there are a number of factors at play. In some cases, your way is genuinely based on new research, which she wasn't party to: the classic example is babies being put to sleep on their back rather than their front. We're right, and they were wrong, and it's a miracle we all survived. Those examples are actually rather rare, though, which is why we always use the one about sleeping position.

Much more plentiful is information which claims to be the final word on the matter, but our mothers have their doubts. Food fads change all the time. When I had my first child, experts used to say that you should separate all tastes, so that they could identify clearly what they were eating. This would make them less likely to be fussy in the future, because they had a sense of agency.

When I had my second child, you were meant to feed them exactly what you were eating, except pureed. These nuggets of advice are clearly contradictory, and were only two years apart (if you've a new baby and are only half-concentrating, can I just underline that I used 'nuggets' metaphorically; you should never puree a nugget for anyone).

The point is that, the more you surround parenting with expertise, and disregard or undermine individual decision-making in favour of a rule-bound approach, then the more irrelevant the previous generation becomes. A woman who raised her child in the '70s has no more to tell you about feeding or bonding or sleeping than a physicist who trained in the '50s could tell you about the Higgs boson. And yet, of course, this is incorrect: parenting is not a science, it will not, and will never, fit into a set of rules, and on some elemental level, everybody can see this. There will be some things we're doing better than the mothers of the past, but there will be other things they did better than us. They don't want to go head-to-head with the prevailing culture, however, and they don't really want to get into a fight with us, especially not when we look so rough and have got breastmilk all over our clothes.

What I find interesting, though I say this only from personal observation, is the way affixing expertise to parenting, even using 'parenting' as this active verb, breaks what should be a natural handing-down of experience from one generation to the next. In a world where every piece of advice is the 'latest' and comes complete with a brain scan, the past has very little to offer you in the way of reassurance. And yet, they take one look at us, our £1,200 buggies, our sleep aids that they can see will never work, and they know we haven't got this all figured out. They know that what we think of as expertise will, in the fullness of time, turn out to have been group hysteria. They suspect that there are other forces at work, perhaps simple market forces, taking advantage of the modern parental propensity to freak out.

What I'm trying to convey (delicately, without causing a fight between you guys) is: when your mother says, 'Darling, are you sure you need an anklet heart beat sensor? We never had one when you were tiny,' she's attempting something bigger: all this money you're spending, this anxiety you're fostering, these rules you're obeying, all this intensity … are you sure it's really necessary? No one would ever say, 'Things were better in my day, we were more sensible and less uptight' – and quite rightly too. Taboos are there for a reason. However, when, in years to come, this atmosphere has relaxed and 'benign neglect' is once again the semi-comic parenting model of choice, we may revisit these delicate questions about our £150 sterilising equipment and appreciate the advice our mothers were really trying to offer: 'Chill out, woman.'

Come back, Superwoman

As for the career-woman taboo – it is not so long ago that we had more complexity in our vision of womanhood. We used to have an ideal of 'Superwoman', the mother who was back in her jeans at six weeks, back at her desk at eight, a powerbroker and dealmaker whose occasional lapses in maternal duties were simply proof of her all-round awesomeness. That wasn't a very realistic portrait of the working mother, it transpired. So far as history relates, the only woman ever to successfully pull it off was Nicola Horlick. But, as Gaby Hinsliff, author of *Half a Wife*, remarked last year:

> What seems to be pitched now is a kind of stealth career, where you are doing something really interesting that you love, but it's not interfering with your life. So instead of Superwoman, we have the mumpreneur, running an organic food empire from her kitchen table in Fulham and then baking all afternoon. And that's not very realistic either.[22]

The salient difference is that the stealth career should never threaten the maternalism. You should continue to pull in money, of course, but you are essentially back to the biologically determined, maternally programmed broodmare that society took you for 100 or 1,000 years ago. It's understandable how this happened; it's an inevitable correction of the career-bitch vibe that held children to be no more than signs of a woman's

---

22 *Guardian* interview with me.

success, accessories to her kick-assery. Yet this correction has over-corrected. Women shouldn't, this century, have to accept a binary narrative, where we're either 'total mother' or 'non-mother'. Do men have to be total fathers, in order to be fathers at all?

Now things become truly ridiculous. As mothers all fervently pretend that work is a necessity, and parenting is the true fulfilment, we then manage to enrage the preceding generation, who find this picture compromised, schmaltzy and weak, a complete derogation of the rights that they fought for. Equality was supposed to be about fighting to achieve what you were capable of, even after you had children – not making your children the thing that you were capable of. Instead, what happened? A generation of women failed to achieve full parity at home, never closed the 'chores gap' with their menfolk, wound themselves into a tight coil of perfectionism and sleep-deprivation, and have taken up the fiction that careers never mattered that much in the first place. Who needs the patriarchy? Women are such pushovers we basically oppress ourselves to save anybody else the trouble.

Then mix in some – I think, legitimate – hostility from non-mothers at the readiness with which mothers have accepted their biological function as their 'main' function, the fulfilment of their genetic legacy as their total, all-encompassing fulfilment. I find it ironic how unsisterly motherhood has become. It is portrayed as the endpoint of the sisterhood, that mothers support one another, and, in order to do so, accept motherhood as a pure goal that supersedes any other goal. But this isn't what sisterhood was supposed to be about at all; it was supposed to be about emancipation, about freeing ourselves – with each other's encouragement – from the constraints that suffocated our potential. While motherhood, from the moment of conception, needs feminism (if we don't want to be mutilated in childbirth and disempowered after it), feminism needs a hell of a lot more than motherhood. In order to say, 'Women are more than wombs,' we have to say, 'People are more than parents.' There is a hard edge to the new sentimentality around parenting, one of judgment against the unnatural non-parent.

Unbelievably, this is again turned into a bitch fight

between the total mother and the non-mother. On each side, feeling the ad hominem derision of the other, tribal allegiance hardens, and that false division becomes the true one. But the real divide is between people who want to see women get an equal shot at self-actualisation, and people who really don't care whether women are fulfilled, just so long as they've cleaned behind the fridge.

And father came too

If this is all one gigantic catfight – generation against generation, rich against poor, huggers against schedulers, stay-at-homes against career bitches, barren against breeders – what of men? Where are men, anyway? Have they just slopey-shouldered the whole thing and gone back to their 'jobs'? (If you're wondering why I put jobs in inverted commas, it's just to underline that I think they are much less like hard work than looking after children.)

Not exactly. This same battle between what you might call, as an umbrella term, the essentialist parent, in which the child is at the centre of all things, and the more sceptical parent, plays out between men too. If you think motherhood is in flux, there's turbulence too among fathers. As Michael Lewis noted in *Home Game*:

> We're in the midst of some long, unhappy transition between the model of fatherhood as practised by my father, and some ideal model, approved by all, to be practised with ease by the perfect fathers of the future. But for now, there's an unsettling absence of universal, or even local, standards of behavior. Within a few miles of my house I can find perfectly sane men and women who regard me as a Neanderthal who should do more to help my poor wife with the kids, and just shut up about it. But I can also find other perfectly sane men and women who view me as a Truly Modern Man and marvel aloud at my ability to be both breadwinner and domestic dervish – doer of an approximately 31.5 per cent of all parenting. The absence of standards is the social equivalent of the absence of an acknowledged fair price for a good in a marketplace. At best, it leads to haggling; at worst, to market failure.[23]

---

23 *Home Game: An Accidental Guide to Fatherhood*, Michael Lewis, W. W. Norton & Co., 2009.

You know when you're a kid fighting with your sister and your parents are constantly telling you off for fighting, even though they're not really listening and they don't realise how much mutual understanding, showmanship, irony and fun there is, underneath your fight? And then *they* turn round and have an absolute blazer of a fight, which reveals in about five seconds the depth of their hatred for one another? This is roughly how I feel when fathers start arguing. I love it.

I know, I know. If you examine this analogy too closely, you'll see mothers cast as the kids, with fathers cast as the authority figures, then you'll see me revelling in discord, even while I've just spent thousands of words bemoaning unnecessary discord. It's none of that: it's simply that women, as soon as we become mothers, have our disputes microscopically scrutinised the whole time. We are made to feel and sound ridiculous for the way we can't just 'get along'. So when fathers, too, find it hard to get along, I feel like I can breathe again, because the truth is punching its way out of this amniotic sac. This isn't a gendered problem. This is a problem that happens when society is saying contradictory things at full volume, controversial things in opaque and sly ways, or ridiculous things without being challenged. When there are no norms, or the norms are wrong, or new norms are being pushed that are just crazy, discourse gets a little feverish. This is not a woman thing.

Fathers have it easy in the early, pre-fatherhood stages – nobody harasses them about their fertility window, even though it also has its limits, and they too will experience disappointment if they don't realise those limits before it's too late. Nobody exaggerates the possible effect of their drinking, smoking, stress or exposure to industrial chemicals. (There is some research on exposure to chemicals or other adverse conditions – like heat – and how it affects fertility. However, the question that is almost never asked is: 'Those damaged sperm that do get through – could they contribute to a damaged foetus?' This is a salient example of how scientific enquiry is, like anything else, built on the foundational prejudices of the culture. Men will be interested in the matter of their virility; nobody is interested in their effect on the foetus because that's the woman's problem.)

There is an expectation, which is, to all intents and purposes, the orthodoxy, that the man will attend the birth. You can tell the age of this tradition (thirty-plus years) by the fact that it's still considered something the father does to support the mother, and hasn't been recast as something a father has to do to prove the intensity of his feeling for the baby.

The contested territories of fatherhood come a bit later, in the large-baby stage. Are you a man or a man-husk? Do you aim for a role that is discrete from the mother's, less involved but more indulgent? Or are you basically exactly the same as a mother, without the breasts? You can see this played out in the pages of men's magazines and weekend supplements. Sometimes it annoys me, as – struggling to articulate what is basically sexism, without sounding sexist – they end up at weak conclusions like, 'My wife is just better at it,' as though there were some gender-coded innate ability to get up in the middle of the night or learn how to fold a buggy. Other times, it is hilarious, as men (some men) still find it much easier than women to articulate how bloody annoying parenthood can be, how tedious it is and how childish children are. The journalist Damon Syson once described the final two hours of a day with a toddler – walking round the house with a nappy in one hand and a corkscrew in the other. Mothers, even the sassy ones, don't say that kind of thing in the public domain (well, except for on blogs).

It's now broadly accepted that the old model of fatherhood – where you ignore your children until they're old enough to go to the pub – is a loss to both you and them. But it's noticeable (well, I've noticed it) that the discussion around the new dad ideal is mainly focused on male identity: whether it is compromised by a caring role; how that compromise is felt; how it can be accommodated or overcome; what the possible pitfalls are for the relationship between the father and the mother. Plus, you still hear quite a lot about what it does to a man's sex life, having children. You rarely hear much about what it does to a woman's sex life, except rueful remarks about how much they'd like to avoid sex. In *Mother, Madonna, Whore: The Idealization and Denigration of Motherhood*, the psychoanalyst Estela Welldon wrote:

In some women, any sexual pleasure related to their breasts ceases not only in pregnancy, but for years after weaning has occurred. This phenomenon has been described to me by many women who experience a tremendous sense of loss when they renew lovemaking with their partners and become aware of this missing dimension that had previously afforded them such erotic excitement.[24]

It's striking that, fewer than twenty years later, this idea is totally absent from the conversation – that a woman might experience loss through breastfeeding, having previously had a sexual identity which included her breasts. Welldon herself alludes to the feminist bookshops that banned her book because they objected to the characterisation of breasts as sexual in the first place. Whatever happened to pro-sex feminism is a conversation for another day. But I would add that the baby-centricity has had a role to play here: if the child is everything, then a mother with sexual urges has missed her memo.

---

24 *Mother, Madonna, Whore: The Idealization and Denigration of Motherhood*, Estela V. Welldon, Karnac Books, 1998.

In consequence, while pre-motherhood, female sexuality is endlessly considered and paraded, with post-motherhood, we've gone back to a quasi-medieval reading of women and sex, in which we do it once a year as a favour or a birthday present.

Sorry – terrible segue from 'What do men think?' to 'How often do mothers want to have sex?'

It's like I have a one-track mind.

Part IV

Part III

Children and the
performance index

T HE FLIP SIDE of the new intensity of parenthood is that children are under quite a lot of pressure to perform, and to be perfect. This was really underlined last year when the conservative MP Liz Truss made two interventions: the first was to suggest a change in guidelines, so that one nursery worker could look after six children under three years old. The second was to bemoan the fact that children in nursery were 'running around with no sense of purpose'. She was quite widely mocked at the time – firstly, because that 1:6 ratio was radically impractical, and secondly, for the idea that two-year-olds ought to have a purpose. But there is a deeper message here. If you attempt, on the one hand, to make economies which mean tiny children get less attention, while on the other hand, you try to interject a sense of 'purpose' into the nursery world, what you're effectively suggesting is less unstructured play – the kind that needs intensive supervision – and more structured 'learning' – which can be undertaken by fewer people. The ideal of making small kids learn more stuff, more quickly, is just a bad faith argument for a change that is basically economic: let's make childcare cheaper by reducing regulation around it.

The early-years curriculum was changed and made more demanding in September 2012. The differences are quite marked: where previously children of four had to count to ten, now they have to 'work confidently with numbers to twenty'. The justification often given for this is that our adult literacy and numeracy rates are actually declining, with people in the 16–24 age group scoring less well than their parents. However, it's not a straightforward equation between stringency of testing and ultimate attainment. Many people who work in adult education – picking up the kids whose core education didn't equip them with adequate skills – say there's too much testing and formal education in the early years, rather than too little. It's at this point that the conversation always turns to Denmark or Finland or the Netherlands. Why can't we be more like them? They always seem so happy.

It is well known that, in countries where the school starting age is seven, people spend longer in voluntary education after school and the population is better educated.[25] So why do we do things the way we do?

Well, this question has a long tail. Pretty much since universal primary school provision was invented, its purpose (stated or unstated) has been to free up parents for work. In the past twenty years, the fiction has grown in such a way that, if the government can refine its targets and tests well enough, all parents need to do is consult a spreadsheet. They will be able to tell instantly which school is best for their child, and that can be the limit of parental involvement (then they can go back to concentrating on work).

---

25 http://news.bbc.co.uk/1/hi/education/7234578.stm; http://www.routledge.com/books/details/9780415548717/

It's an absolute fiction. First, 'choice' doesn't mean choice, does it? All parents want the same thing: an environment in which their child will be challenged yet cared for. So what they call 'choice' is really a scramble, as every parent tries to get their children into the same schools, where challenge and care are deemed, by some coarse metric, to be the best. Second, kids only spend 12 per cent of their waking time in school. To try and map the quality and nature of a school using the data of the achievements of its pupils is just too blunt. It might tell you something, but it can't tell you everything. It's like trying to gauge the nutritional quality of a restaurant by the weight of its customers. Sure, they probably like a bit of lard otherwise they wouldn't be in Ed's Diner in the first place. But how do you know what they eat at home? Third, the targets force a very strangulated, narrow agenda: you just can't take any risks with Key Stages and SATs. Whatever you believe about the necessity of breadth and experiment, and the importance of learning things that aren't necessarily instantly applicable in the job market, you can't take the risk with your child's school's reputation. But fourth, and most importantly, this pressure on children to achieve, rather than simply be, is enormous. The irony is that private schools, once considered superior for their results, are now trumpeted as the only place to send your child if you want them to have any breadth in their learning, any looseness, any music, any sport. We've reached a point where, if you want some respite for your child from academic pressure, you have to buy your way out of the system.

This extends beyond school into all their waking hours – the onus upon self-improvement is huge for children. Grandparents look on, baffled, as we fill our children's weekends and after-school hours with extra maths, endless arcane sports, philosophy, skills that we wouldn't dream of trying to accrue ourselves. It reminds me of John O'Farrell, musing on Radio 4 about the impossibility of getting teenagers out to a museum. He has an epiphany halfway through: 'Hang on – *I* don't want to go to a museum either. I just want to lie on the sofa and read the paper.'

In practice, even though I disagree with all this fervently, I still buy into it with my kids. I still make them do their homework; I'd still be upset if they fell behind;

it still matters to me whether or not they're meeting their early years goals, whether they're expected or emergent or exceeding. So when I quote this, from *Psychology Today*, an American online magazine, it is not gleefully, but with enormous guilt:

> Imagine a job in which your work every day is micromanaged by your boss. You are told exactly what to do, how to do it, and when to do it. You are required to stay in your seat until your boss says you can move. Each piece of your work is evaluated and compared, every day, with the work done by your fellow employees. You are rarely trusted to make your own decisions. Research on employment shows that this is not only the most tedious employment situation, but also the most stressful. Micromanagement drives people crazy.
>
> Kids are people, and they respond just as adults do to micromanagement, to severe restrictions on their freedom, and to constant, unsolicited evaluation. School, too often, is exactly like the kind of nightmare job that I just described; and, worse, it is a job that kids are not allowed to quit. No matter how much they might be suffering,

they are forced to continue, unless they have enlight-
ened parents who have the means, know-how and will
to get them out of it. Including homework, the hours are
often more than those that their parents put into their
full-time jobs, and freedom of movement for children
at school is far less than that for their parents at work.[26]

The author, Peter Gray, was précising his findings about
emergency admissions for children to psychiatric units.
His hypothesis was that school is extremely stressful,
and, therefore, over the summer months, such episodes
would decrease. What he found was a drop of nearly
two-thirds – 185 admissions in May, only sixty-six in
August. Now, clearly, that's a pretty small sample, but
the criteria were very tight: he was only counting cases
that were serious enough to require an overnight stay, or
longer. If you had more than 185 kids attending one hospital (the Connecticut Children's Medical Centre) in one
month, and needing to stay overnight, you would think

---

26 'The Danger of Back to School', Peter Gray, *Psychology Today*, 7 August
2014.

you had a pretty major problem on your hands. Even a problem of this magnitude is pretty severe, let's face it.

Naturally, this is America; their school system is different to ours, we cannot look at it as a direct indication of what happens here. Yet we can look at our own system and see likenesses. Kids are constantly tested, from a very young age. We never test their happiness; we never try and fashion an unhappiness index. Teachers try to shield them from the pressure, but all kids know what's going on. Every school policy, right down to Nick Clegg's free school meals for all (so long as you're five, six or seven), is presented as a way to assist concentration. Even playtime now has to be framed as the fulfilment of some goal or other, whether it's an anti-obesity goal or the goal of letting off steam in order to learn better. Teachers themselves are rolled into the targets, assessed and marked and graded in a way that cannot possibly reflect their full, rounded selves. In what other job do people accept being ranked into one of four bands? In what other job would someone have to say, 'I'm an outstanding,' or 'I'm a satisfactory'? In a brilliant anonymous blog, one head of department noted:

The words have been bastardised beyond belief.

'Outstanding': passable – everyone should be this.

'Good': not good enough, you need to improve to be outstanding.

'Requires improvement': terrible.

'Inadequate': really terrible, resign now, you loser.

Sure, there's an argument that teachers are grown-ups and can look after themselves. But what this all adds up to is an atmosphere of intense scrutiny and assessment that our kids have to live in, all day. The best headteachers in the country are the ones who can absorb all these targets and not pass that pressure onto the kids and the teachers. And there are, mercifully, hundreds of heads who manage that.

But to whose advantage is all of this? It strikes me that it's a politically devised system for politicians – who, by and large, have the least experience of state education, and the smallest stake in it – to wave their successful targets at one another. And beneath that there is the fact that, if you turn parenting into something expertise-based, in which there is a right way and thousands of wrong ways, in which the raw truth of it – idiosyncratic human beings loving each other in their own particular ways – is airbrushed out, then you end up doing a lot of counting. You count their weight and their height and their progress and their market-readiness; you count their sociability and their vocabulary and their fitness. And all of this, for the kids being counted, is punishing. In the midst of all the inequalities that we live with, we've managed to create one level playing field between rich and poor: the kids in private schools are as anxious as the kids in failing schools. We've managed to create an environment so scrutinised that it equalises all our children in unhappiness.

The last time the government collected national prevalence data on youth mental health was in 2004, so there's a real problem pinning down what this is doing to young people. However, it is pretty plain from the pressure on services that childhood anxiety is increasing, and it is inconceivable that this would be unrelated to the pressure children face at school and beyond. Self-harm is now a huge thing among teenagers: one in twelve children deliberately harm themselves; 25,000 kids a year end up in hospital as a result. In the '80s, this was almost unheard of.

Meanwhile, that intense risk-sensitivity observed in pregnancy and early years continues – everything is framed as a risk to one's children. They start making bracelets out of loom bands, and they are suddenly 'doom bands'. (After a boy fell asleep with some round his fingers, and cut off his circulation. Also, another boy was hit in the eye with one and suffered a blood clot. Both these incidents are unfortunate but, you've got to admit, could occur following the misuse of any small piece of elastic, or, in the second case, any small projectile.)[27]

The determination to find a brain tumour link to mobile phone use is, I think, going to persist until long after we've stopped using phones and have mini-data terminals implanted onto our retinas. The parameters of what children should be allowed to do by themselves has completely changed: they can't walk to school alone, let alone cycle;[28] a mother was given a police caution for

---

27 http://www.dailymail.co.uk/news/article-2686823/
    Loom-bands-health-risk-says-GP-Parents-told-craze-damage-childrens-
    circulation-schools-introduce-bans.html

28 http://john-adams.co.uk/wp-content/uploads/2007/11/one%20false%20
    move.pdf; http://www.psi.org.uk/images/uploads/Briefing-Childrens_
    Independent_Mobility_v4_3.pdf

letting her nine-year-old go to the playground alone. This trend is much more advanced and amplified in America, where bitter public fights about child safety occur and the voice of 'caution' very often advocates jail sentences for parents who fail to abide by rules which, in the '70s, would have been considered neurotic. It is astonishing to consider that, in 1971, two years before I was born, 86 per cent of parents let their primary-aged children come home from school on their own. That figure is now 25 per cent,[29] but the more 'lax' parents (as they're now considered) are under a pall of suspicion. A couple who allowed their children to cycle to school in 2010 were referred to the social services.[30]

An interesting experiment – in groups of families, or even just within your own – is to try and figure out how many unsupervised minutes your kids have had in their lives. Just time to themselves, without an adult in hearing distance. My children are six and five, and I'd say

---

29 'The demise of the free-range child', John Adams: http://www.john-adams.co.uk/2007/12/07/the-demise-of-the-free-range-child/

30 http://www.telegraph.co.uk/news/uknews/7871046/Couple-warned-over-allowing-children-to-cycle-to-school-alone.html

they've had none. That said, my daughter and her friend pulled a bathroom door off its hinges while I was supervising them when they were four. So I must admit that the intensity of my supervision is not very high.

What is really obvious – or should be – is a lack of basic human wisdom here. Neurosis feeds off itself and finds its image in others. You can supervise children for every waking minute, you can reduce to almost nothing the number of things they're allowed to do alone, but you cannot expect that to be completely without consequence. It may reduce the risk of the outlying event – abduction by a paedophile, for instance – but it will create risks of its own. What's becoming plain is that, not only does this not really improve their safety – the danger from strangers being a very minor threat against the danger posed by family members – but it actually has its costs. Strangers who are well-meaning (which, let's not forget, most of them are) no longer feel able to interact with children. If you saw a child in the street and wanted to say something like, 'What's the matter?' (if they were crying) or, 'Nice bike!' (if they had a new bike), you would need the qualification of your own children accompanying you in order to not look like a weirdo. So children, steadily, learn that the only trustworthy adults are those who are demonstrably parents, and everybody else should be approached with a prefixed distrust. Add to that the fact that, in life, they are simply untested – not allowed to go off alone, make mistakes and come back – while in education, they are over-tested, and anxiety becomes natural. Who could exist in these conditions and not be anxious?

Ultimately, we're back to risk – hazards that were once considered part of life are no longer acceptable, either for mothers-to-be, new mothers, old mothers, fathers or children. The landscape has come to be shaped by the avoidance of risk. I remember discussing this with Ellie Lee, sociologist at Kent University.[31] She said that it's what happens when politics ceases to be about progress; when history announces itself to have ended; when ide-

---

31 People sometimes call her a disciple of Frank Furedi, looking to discredit her ideas with the link. I actually like his work too, and don't accept that the association is discrediting. But it annoys me that it's bloody sexist. She's younger than him and female, in the same department, at the same university. But she's not his disciple.

ology is declared over: 'If you're not going anywhere, if you're not headed towards something better, then you become preoccupied with maintaining the present. Not improving it, protecting it from threat.'

I agree, but I also, over the past seven years of being a parent or nearly a parent, think there's something else. It's very socially bonding, having children. It's hard not to empathise with someone whose children are the same age as yours or younger. Whether they're Palestinian mothers whose sons have been killed while they played, or fathers in Sainsbury's whose toddlers are having a meltdown, it's hard not to get a flash of what they're feeling, and it gives lie to the idea that we're all purely self-interested and at our most productive when we're looking after our own. In fact, we're magnetically drawn to each other, and never feel more alive than when we can look at a stranger and step inside their skin, even for a second.

A lot of the architecture of society – the health service, the safety net, the bald fact that we wouldn't be happy to let one another starve – is based on that fellow feeling. You rarely have to think, 'How would I feel, if that happened to me?' when you read a story about a mother with small kids being made homeless, or a family visiting a foodbank; you know immediately how you would feel, and you know immediately what you want society to look like. You want it to look like a place where those things don't happen to anyone.

The thrust away from dumb luck and towards individual responsibility is really an attack on empathy. If everything has an individual cause, you don't have to sympathise with that mother whose child is disabled – she probably didn't eat the right vitamins while she was pregnant. You don't have to have fellow feeling when that child was hit by a car – that child should never have been outside the house, that child was unsupervised. You don't have to feel for those parents whose child is self-harming or anorexic – they probably put it in nursery when it was too young, and are now witnessing the consequences of its cortisol levels.

But we all know, by the evidence of our own five senses, that this is not how it works, that the world can be cruel for reasons unrelated to frivolous or irresponsible behaviour. We know that our empathy is not misplaced, and, furthermore, that it is a much more fulfilling and fecund emotion than just scratching around to apportion blame. We all know that tiny, sterile, risk-free family units with the child as their miniature emperor are a horrible substitute for a wider environment that cares about children and adults alike.

When we retake what we all know childhood to be – a social endeavour – then we can become the village that knows how to raise a child.

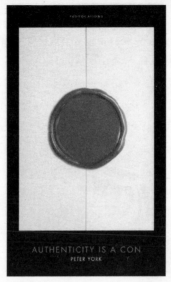